How to Become Wealthy

The Essential Guide to Becoming Rich While You're Still Young Enough to Enjoy It

by William Reese

Table of Contents

Introduction

Welcome to the 21st century—the golden times of prosperity and futuristic living. Well, that's what generations X, Y, and the rest of the millennials are expecting anyway. ***Reality check:*** The cost of living outstrips most blue collar and white collar incomes; you can't take a step anywhere without landing in debt and loans; the most basic pleasures in life leave a hole in your pocket; the return value from brand-name educational degrees isn't the same as it once was; and market competition in every field is cut-throat and brutal.

But here's the thing....

At the same time, never before have we seen as many youngsters and twenty-somethings entering the ranks of ***millionaires*** as we have in recent years. What exactly makes that possible? Not all of them have a mind like Zuckerberg's, so how does a person without any brilliant flash of inspiration or without a game-changing product make a ton of money? Well, first of all, they understand the difference between being *rich* and being *wealthy*—and **yes**, there's a vast chasm spanning between the two which will be discussed in detail in the next chapter.

Getting back on topic, becoming a millionaire isn't nearly as complicated or difficult as it's made out to be. In fact, it's rather simple. However, the objective truth remains that while becoming wealthy and getting slimmer through dieting and exercise are both *simple*, that still doesn't mean it is *easy*. And therein lies the catch.

To make things just a little bit easier, this book was written as a fool-proof guide to simplifying your needs, straightening your path to financial freedom, and shining a light on a tried-and-tested way to get you to millionaire-dom, and all while you're still young enough to actually enjoy it!

So what do you say? Are you ready to grasp the intricacies of financial freedom with your own two hands and take charge of your future prosperity? Are you prepared to open yourself to the awe-inspiring world of millionaires, and lead your life as you see fit, free of financial obligations by the time you leave your 20s or early 30s? Then let's get started!

Chapter 1: Being Wealthy vs. Being Rich

As I mentioned in the introduction, there's a vast chasm between the states of wealth and riches, and that chasm is often called poverty. Confused? Well, put simply, rich people are never wealthy, while wealthy people are never rich. And I'm sure that didn't help the confusion in the matter.

To understand this better, let's compare both states and what the world means by them. The state of being rich is often equated with having large sums of cash on hand, or liquid assets, which are then used frequently and generously in order to solve any obstacle, discomfort, inconvenience, or annoyance that may come across the path of the rich—like driving like morons because they know they can afford tickets if caught, or the inconvenience of having to eat plain and healthy food when take-out can be ordered in from that famous sushi restaurant across town.

However, rich people don't *stay* rich very often, and are frequent visitors to poor-town, even if their expenses and outward behavior doesn't always say so. That's because, no matter how much you earn every month, if your expenses far outstrip your income or even just *barely* fall under the amount of incoming money, you'll never have any soft padded cushions for when life kicks you off the airplane of luxury mid-flight. You'll land on the hard, cold ground of reality, and will probably never be able to get up again. Moreover, even if you manage to maintain a constant rate of income, and your expenses always *just* fall within the influx amount, you're about one tragedy, one health issue, or even a fall in earnings away from poor-town.

Before we move on further, let me clarify one thing— I don't use the phrase "poor-town" like the British would describe "the great unwashed". In fact, there are hundreds and thousands of low-income households that could be described as wealthy, even though they are without complete financial freedom. Such low-income households may depend on their primary earners more than truly wealthy households, and may not be able to buy the best life insurance or the latest iPad's, but they won't ever go hungry either. Instead, "poor-town" is used to describe a mentality where your expenses have far outstripped your income, and now you don't have an income to support said lifestyle anymore. Yet, several elements of that lifestyle cannot be negotiated or simply cut down, and so you're faced with abject poverty—zero income, titanic expenses.

The people of "rich-town" are always concerned with short-term comforts, and often make excuses to justify their needs and necessities. They focus solely on increasing the amounts of money that they need to bring in to consolidate their exorbitant lifestyles, or simply refuse to face the necessity of compromise in life's expectations and rewards. Then, when they hit an income ceiling, and yet their expenses keep growing because of their utter lack of discipline, they revert to "poor-town", and the harsh teachings of life are force-fed to them.

On the other hand is the grand country of "Wealthytopia" whose population may be a couple of hundred thousand out of seven billion humans on Earth. Let's get one thing clear, these people may have an annual income of some thousands, or hundreds of thousands, or even millions. Regardless, they'll never grace "poor-town" with their presence. Why? Because they know the difficulties of that life. For many years and decades, they would have *already* been treating themselves as poor even if they made a lot of money. They've sacrificed comforts for future freedom, replaced the sack of money solving their problems with thorough preparedness, and are able to stand on their own two feet without ever needing someone else's help or financial support. Such people aren't just pragmatists—because you *need* to be a dreamer to become wealthy. You *need* to know your endgame so that you can dedicate your life to reaching that goal. And again, by endgame, I don't mean that VP seat on the tech company you're working for, or that cushy board of directors' chamber in whichever firm you slave away. The endgame is simple—even if I *do* continue working after I'm 35, or 40, or 45, it will *only* be because I **choose** to do so in order to stay productive, rather than compulsively *having* to work because I'll go bankrupt without my monthly paycheck.

And yes, I'm well aware that "Wealthytopia" has a utopian element—in essence, a dream which never *completely* realizes exactly how it's envisioned. Because that's the *other* secret that wealthy people come to terms with on this journey. While you may have started on the journey to becoming wealthy with the image of rolling around in money without having to work, and playing in expensive cars and luxurious homes, you *will* have to prioritize your needs on the way there. That's because, and you'll only agree with me on this when you're halfway there—the *luxury* of not having to worry about monthly bills and incomes, whether you work or not, **always** beats the luxury of eating in a fancy restaurant every day. So, even when you're wealthy and you have the money to be able to do so, the change in your character along this path will be so ingrained that you won't *want* to spend unnecessarily and without a great reason behind every expense. Therefore, the people of Wealthytopia will always remain hard-working, financially savvy, productive, and self-sustaining members of society. While they may not always rank in the Forbes top 100 lists, they will certainly never care about whether there's enough money in the bank or not.

Again, there's a point which needs clarifying—being wealthy doesn't mean that you need to be a miserly penny pincher. It means that you develop an understanding of the true worth of every cent you spend. It symbolizes reaching a point where you can responsibly decide whether an expense is worth it or not. It doesn't mean that you never go out and eat in a fancy restaurant, or watch that movie or play. It means that you reserve your money for the outings that you or your loved ones would *truly* appreciate from the bottom of all your hearts, and *maybe* reserving a trip to that fancy restaurant when you wish to treat friends, family, or other people you care about so that the occasion is special in more ways than blind expenditure. So, being wealthy means having the necessary *sense* to be able to sacrifice convenience and comfort where you can, to be able to enjoy other greater pleasures in life—like an amazingly developed house just big enough for your needs in a mind-blowing location that you've always admired, rather than spending that same money on 1000 trips to that mid-range restaurant over the next two decades.

As I mentioned, becoming wealthy *is* simple—all it needs is that you *don't* spend unnecessarily on acquiring the latest gadgets and clothes, and instead make smart decisions on waiting and buying things that you *need* when their price drops to reasonable amounts for starters—but it's not *easy*. It requires dedication, diligence, a long term vision, and tremendous sacrifice. But, do this for the next ten or fifteen years, even if you do almost nothing else, and you'll be far ahead of others in the same age range as you—and possibly, even those older.

Chapter 2: Making a Game Plan

If you can't dream, you can't get wealthy. That's a bitter truth. However, when I say that you need to have a dream, I don't mean "I wish to become NYC's most-celebrated author by 35", but rather something along the lines of "I want to earn my first million within the next six years". Basically, I mean a financial target that you wish to achieve, for whatever reason.

So, for starters, you need to do your homework, chalk out your dream, and construct a game plan. This needs to be *written down*. A single sentence on a huge chart, a piece of paper or banner, displayed in a way so it's the first thing you see every morning. Possibly right opposite to your bed in your room. As cheesy as this may sound, it's going to play a large part in keeping up your motivation and drive.

A study which attempted to determine the power of written goals in a company unearthed that only 3% within the study group created written long-term action plans and motivations, and these people were 10 times more likely to achieve their objectives than those who didn't write them down. The reason

15

behind it is quite straight forward. While the human mind is perfectly capable of retaining objectives, it loses the motivation and intensity of emotion linked to that goal as time progresses. This wear-and-tear of motivation is further sped up by obstacles, inconveniences, and easy ways out—all of which apply on the path to Wealthytopia. Also, without a single foci which concentrates all the memories of sacrifice, diligence, and work you've put into your goal so far, it's easy to forget the hardships you've put in and head back to the easy path.

When you write down your goals in a prominent manner while the memory of the motivation is still fresh in your mind, you're also imbuing your writing with the memory of that motivation. Thus, whenever you look at that poster or banner with "I'm going to create my first million within the next six years", your mind will automatically reverberate with the memories of the original motivation, and every sacrifice, discomfort, inconvenience, and downright hardship which you've undergone in order to bring your dream come true. It will straighten your spine each morning, and serve as a support whenever the going gets truly hard and you need to put yourself through further pain in the short-term to reach your long-term objectives.

Going back to practical matters, when you're formulating your game plan, you need to research the city, state, or country in which you wish to reside within the next five or six years. If the place you wish to head to, or where your job might take you, is *more* expensive than the one where you live right now—you may need to tighten your belt further in order to meet your target. But, this can only be achieved when you *already* plan for how much ever of your life can be predicted. Of course, your office could ask you to move to Singapore or Japan out of the blue, and you will have to adjust accordingly as you go along—the point being that you can't possibly plan for *every* eventuality. However, within what is known to you, preparing a plan which is as detailed as possible will help you tremendously in creating a survivable environment where you can get your needs and *just enough* comforts met to get by, without completely breaking down along the way.

You'll also have to figure out, based on your current income (and adjusting for inflation over the next five years), the figure which you'll need to save up at the minimum in order to reach your goals. Along with this, you'll also have to identify different areas where you can boost the value of your income, with ways that we'll discuss in the subsequent chapters.

Chapter 3: Reducing Your Expenses

The first and *most important* step to Wealthytopia is to cut down your expenses. And this doesn't just mean trimming out comforts. It means cutting out comforts, taking on inconveniences, and *then* some. I can already hear the excuses bubbling out of you readers: "I barely go to movies or parties, and almost never eat outside. The only luxuries I allow myself are X, Y and Z". Yes, yes, I know. I've heard every variation of this excuse and had repeated several of them to myself over the years. However, I didn't understand the value of financial freedom until I let go of all of said excuses, and started treating nothing but the barest expenses on my food, and those for my studies and work as pure necessities. Absolutely everything was an extra. For those of you who also need to care for others, or may have added responsibilities—I had a partner through all this who made the same sacrifices as I did, so that we could both look forward to a prosperous future just six or seven years down the line.

So, understand that every time you look at your clothes and think "Hmm, I've been wearing this for two years. Maybe I need to upgrade..." - even *that* is a luxury: a "want", not a "need". It doesn't turn into a need 'til your clothes wear through with holes, and you need to replace them in order to maintain a presentable appearance. That single bucket of popcorn to which you treat yourself at the movies isn't a necessity, it's a luxury. The biggest enemy that you face on this journey isn't "Oh, let me buy this awesome expensive car," or "I only eat outside everyday to save up on effort". It's the small things here and there—the extra $2 to spend on upsizing your meal, or the $15 more that would let you purchase that perfect top or shirt. These small expenses will be the biggest test of your endurance, and the ones which you need to stay away from the most—because they add up to significant amounts over the year, when every little bit counts towards reaching your goals. Again, it's simple but not *easy*.

So, go through your expenses again, and change your perspective drastically. The question is no longer whether you can live with or without a certain expense, but whether you *should* be living with that expense in your situation. One example in particular is your living arrangements. If you're living in a larger and comfortable apartment alone, consider moving into a smaller space or getting a roommate to cut down on expenses. This single move may increase inconvenience and discomfort for you, but will free up significant amounts of money which can be put to profitable use elsewhere.

Moreover, if you don't eat outside at all, and just purchase groceries so that you can cook at home—either try switching to places where you can get said groceries for cheaper, like dawn-time farmers' markets instead of grocery stores, or try to cut down on your intake 'til you have enough to eat healthy without indulging yourself in food. These changes may seem quite drastic and spartan, and you will face enormous difficulties to overcome a state of mind which tries to defend a "I'm only spending as much as I need and nothing more, so why should I cut down further?" attitude—but it's better than facing citizenship in "poor-town" in a few years, which is where you'll be headed unless you make these changes.

This isn't a scare tactic but a fact—with the rates of inflation as they stand, simply maintaining your idea of a "bare minimum" life will tax you severely in the next half decade or more. Therefore, instead of getting accustomed to a certain standard of living, you need to get used to the idea of living at bare bottom so that your money can rest safely in your hands instead of constantly flowing in and out.

Other ways of cutting down expenses includes figuring out transportation to and from your place of work or studies. If you have a car, to begin with, sell it! You're spending a lot of money each year on its upkeep and fuel costs. Instead, try and figure out the cheapest public transport options, even if they require that you stabilize a fixed routine to accommodate traveling by buses, subways, trains, etc. If your destinations are close enough, walk! Or get yourself a bicycle for both long and short distances. It will keep you healthy, reduce any gym or healthcare related costs over the next five to seven years, and provide you with various benefits that would have necessitated extra costs otherwise.

Another thing to keep in mind is loans and debts. If you've kept away from them so far, that's great! Stick along this path, and never take out a loan—regardless of how big or small your need may be. Never aim to purchase something which is far outside your means, regardless of value. If you *do* have previous loans, cut out any luxury and leisure—including dating if you don't have a serious partner already—until you're able to repay all your loans first. Nothing strips away financial independence worse than having to pay off loans to formal institutions. If you hit a speed bump and are late with payments, you're slapped with fines. If you land in trouble and can't pay it back, you'll lose far more than the original monetary value which you borrowed. Be on your guard for the insidious danger of getting mired in the credit system. While it provides a convenient path to achieve material goals faster, that convenience comes with a hefty ball and chain that you'll have to lug along for a significant portion of your foreseeable future.

Lastly, if you have pets, as hard as this may be— figure out if you are in the best position to care for another life as you stand right now. This may be harsh to hear, or even think about, and your answer depends on your own attachment to them versus your attachment to your long term goals. It may be that you choose to keep them, and shoulder whatever extra responsibilities they bring, in exchange for reaching your dreams a little later. However, this is a conscious decision that must be made and accepted from an objective point of view, rather than an emotional attachment.

It's perfectly acceptable if you do choose to keep pets like I did—but the value of making a conscious decision rather than treating them as a necessity is what separates you from spendthrift "rich-town" citizens. It forces you to stand up and take account of all the expenses which you *choose* to shoulder as an adult who is responsible for his/her own life, rather than mask responsibilities under the mantle of "necessities".

Chapter 4: Creating a Nest Egg

Let me describe a situation to you: it could also be that you hold yourself to the barest of necessities, and yet never manage to save any significant amounts through the months. As validated as your expense account may be, it's an unfortunate but accurate truth that you still need to create savings if you're to move at all in any direction in your life. Regardless of whether necessities may be large or small in your future, if you can't save up, then you're setting yourself up for failure right off the bat.

Yet, it's hard to understand and distinguish between necessary and unnecessary expenses when your money's easily available and sitting in front of you. Therefore, here's an easy method to ensure that you leave your savings be, instead of plundering them at every given opportunity.

Open up a secondary savings bank account, and don't link any ATM or credit cards to it. Instead, get a check book for said account, enable it for purchases on the stock market—only viable as an option if you're an adult in the eyes of the law—and set up an automatic transfer for 25% of your monthly salary from your regular account to this new one. With this method, 25% of your income will automatically be added to your savings account, and it will still be accessible if needed through checks. However, the inconvenience that it adds will always ensure that you think twice about the necessity of your expenses rather than taking them for granted. Moreover, use the remaining 75% to first get rid of all unavoidable expenses in a month—debts, loans, etc. before you even think of touching the other 25%.

Even if you absolutely *need* to withdraw some money out of this account once in a blue moon, the rest of the sum will still accumulate to larger figures, and will give you a soft bed of support in really hard times, or protect you from unexpected kicks between the legs from the trickster called life. The sooner you can build your "nest egg", so to speak, the faster you can capitalize upon all the wonderful opportunities that the convoluted financial world has to offer.

We won't advise you to leave that 25% in the account itself, collecting meager interests through the account. It will play a pivotal part in the next step of your path to Wealthytopia—without which you will *never* reach your dreams.

Chapter 5: How to Invest Wisely

This is where you'll learn to make the most of that 25% which is auto-added to your savings account each month. The first order of business is to use that money and get yourself some decent insurance—at the very least, medical insurance for starters. Healthcare is an expensive process these days, and you don't want the sniffles to burn through your precious 25% savings, after all that pain and sacrifice.

Once you've spent on insurance, and are setting aside the requisite monthly or annual premium amounts, your next order of business is to build your investment portfolio. Within this, you need to ensure that your money is spread out diversely in secure investments so as to reduce the risk of your savings tanking when a single golden goose takes the dive.

The next order of business is to figure out your 401(k). If you're working for a corporate employer, chances are that you've been offered a few plans outlining pension deposits and growth. Moreover, you've been offered by your employer that each dollar which you deposit in the plan will be matched with 50 cents or a dollar from the employer as well. However, since it's complicated, and there are several pages of financial jargon to go through, you've been pushing it off day after day, promising yourself to complete it on a fabled "tomorrow" which never seems to arrive. That needs to stop right now! Think of the amount of money you miss out on from not capitalizing upon your employers' pledge of adding half the amount or even the full amount which you put into these plans. This money will set you up for your retirement years without having to worry about your financial situation in those times. Since you're already living a spartan life now, and are thus released from worries further on in your life, the only part that's left for you to take care of is your middle age. Now, some pension funds operate on a minimum time basis and can be accessed after five years of starting them—thus leaving you able to utilize their bounty by the time you hit your early thirties and forties and not having to wait till your sixties.

However, we must also take into account the large growth of freelancers and self-employed professionals in this day and age. In many companies, you have the option to set up auto-deductions from your paycheck once you pick your plan. However, none of those options exist for people who work for themselves, which means that you have greater responsibilities to maintaining your own discipline on your own shoulders. In such cases, you need to research and opt for retirement plans directly from their source, and you alone are responsible for monthly deposits into the plan. On the plus side, some plans offer auto-matching of the cost of premiums up to certain limits, either by the government or other private bodies. This will allow you access to the same benefits available to people working under employers, without the downsides that stem from being chained to firms.

The last order of business, of course, is to set up your investments. Essentially, these are in the form of bonds, shares, or real estate. Now, while real estate was traditionally held to be a low-risk, long-term yield investment option, the 2008 bubble proved that no option is entirely secure. In light of that observation, while we keep in mind that the real estate market may yet again be stabilizing and that it's unlikely that we'll see another full scale meltdown anytime soon, you also need to ask yourself—do you really want to invest in real estate? Of course, this excludes owning your own house, which removes the necessity to pay rent every month and provides another step to financial freedom. But, what I speak of is that additional investment in another house, parcel of land, development project, etc.

The one point which people never think about with real estate is that it requires you to keep working as a landlord even after you've achieved financial freedom and have retired. It requires you to have the acumen of a business person, and needs constant maintenance and upkeep to retain the value of your investment. Also, it necessitates being grounded in a certain location so that you can nurture and grow your original investment, unlike shares or bonds which can be mostly managed from any corner of the planet.

After you've figured out your stance on real estate, turn your eye to shares and bonds. Out of the two, bonds are great for nurturing a nest egg for large foreseeable expenses in the future—like saving to buy your own house or your kids' college expenses. Since it's a low risk-low yield investment, it allows you some return while giving you a disciplined way of building up that money which you won't be able to touch for a certain number of years.

Lastly, we come to shares. Now, for first time investors, it's not a bad idea to join a mutual fund or other group investments with reputable firms while you figure out the literature, and gain an understanding of the market on your own merit. However, since most reputable mutual funds have minimum limits which may be inaccessible for you if you've just started earning, it would be best to start investing small amounts on the market instead of just sitting and twiddling your thumbs. Remember that the true magic of investing lies in the mathematical miracle of compound interest, which needs time more than anything to display its true bounties. Therefore, start with smaller investments right off the bat, and put whatever little profit you gather right back into your investments. This will allow the size of your portfolio to grow faster, with portions of your monthly 25% as well as your profits going right back into purchasing further shares for future growth.

While this may be a scary step at first, you can negate undue risk by giving yourself a week to read up as much on investment strategies as you possibly can. Once you've gotten a hang of the ideal investor's mindset, you need to figure out which companies have been performing reasonably consistently without large up or down swings. These companies may not offer a great deal of profit in the short term, but will definitely allow you to make smaller profits and grow your net investment size with a solid foundation. After the week is up, push yourself to at least purchase some stocks of any value no matter what. It's this first step that's always hard to take, and which is met with the most excuses.

Once you've overcome this hurdle, it will become far easier—I guarantee it. Always remember that your portfolio may take hits from time to time, but never panic and make hasty short term decisions. Trust long term performance and trends over short term media or market fluctuations. The best investors *never* trade shares from day to day, and only adjust their portfolios a few times a year. Once you've grown your portfolio enough, figure out ways to spread investments on the international market as well. Doing so will actually *reduce* the risk of your overall portfolio taking a large hit if a single country's economy goes bonkers again.

Conclusion

While making sacrifices and reducing expenses are the building blocks to Wealthytopia—the most important step lies in the disbursal of your money through investments. Each time you deny yourself an ice cream, and instead invest that dollar and a half into another company, you've essentially created a system where that dollar will double its worth for you in the next seven years or so. Therefore, whenever you deny yourself some comfort, keep your eye for the long term growth on the horizon—it will give you strength, and make this journey easier.

Being wealthy isn't just about differentiating between needs and wants, it also relies on reducing unnecessary surprises. Again, this doesn't mean that you don't take any risks with your life, but that you research any path as much as you reasonably can before making a decision—that's the only way any adult can live a wholesome yet secure life, an understanding which many adults unfortunately lack.

On the whole, your next decade may be fraught with hardships. However, take solace in the fact that most of these will be self-inflicted for a greater purpose. Since it becomes quite difficult to justify going through difficulties when the solution for it lies within arm's reach, you either need to keep yourself on track by looking at examples from around your life where people have used similar approaches and succeeded, or ones where they refused to grow up and take charge of their lives and so invariably failed. Becoming wealthy isn't child's play—which is why there have never been wealthy children, only rich ones at best who often saw their way to "poor-town". Being able to understand and accept this responsibility over finances is what separates a child from a mature adult anyway, not age.

In the end, keep this in mind—this isn't an ideal set up, created but never enforced or followed. This is a plan which has been formulated and stuck to by many, *many* people who now grace the lists of millionaires. They have followed these same footsteps, and have seen their way clear to complete financial freedom and, for several thousands of them, even early retirement whilst in their 30s. If they could do it, so can you!

Finally, I'd like to thank you for purchasing this book! If you enjoyed it or found it helpful, I'd greatly appreciate it if you'd take a moment to leave a review on Amazon. Thank you!

Printed in Great Britain
by Amazon

33125360R00026